SPEL... IS A
FOUR-LETTER WORD

J. Richard Gentry

Scholastic

Scholastic-TAB Publications Ltd.
123 Newkirk Road, Richmond Hill, Ontario, Canada L4C 3G5

Scholastic Inc.
730 Broadway, New York, NY 10003, USA

Ashton Scholastic Limited
165 Marua Road, Panmure, PO Box 12328, Auckland 6, New Zealand

Ashton Scholastic Pty Limited
PO Box 579, Gosford, NSW, 2250, Australia

Scholastic Publications Ltd.
Holly Walk, Leamington Spa, Warwickshire CV32 4LS, England

Design by Kathryn Cole

Cover photo © Masterfile/John de Visser

6 5 4 3   Printed in Hong Kong   8 9/8

Canadian Cataloguing in Publication Data

Gentry, J. Richard

  Spel. . . is a four-letter word

(Bright idea)
ISBN 0-590-71685-9

1. English language — Orthography and spelling — Study and teaching.   2. Spelling ability.   I. Title. II. Series.

LB1574.G46 1987   372.6'32   C86-094873-0

Contents

Dear Professor Henderson

You don't remember me. We met in 1969 when I was a sophomore in your Introduction to Shakespeare class. I sensed then that you cared about your students, so you will be pleased to learn that I am successful and happy. Following your lead, I am whittling away at a career as college professor.

You and I shared an experience that may seem trivial after seventeen years, but you know that teachers have a powerful impact on the lives of their students — a small beginning ripple may swell over the years. You created a ripple when we last met, in your office.

It had started in class. After returning essay examinations to the other seventy-eight students, but not to me, you announced, ''Mr. Gentry, please see me in my office.'' Your words sent ice up my spine. I knew I had mastered the materials, and I had never cheated on any test in fourteen years of schooling. Not knowing what the problem was made me settle uncomfortably in the chair next to your desk.

The problem was my spelling.

''Mr. Gentry, you understand Shakespeare. This is an excellent examination. You are one of nine students who have earned an A in my course this semester. But I've asked you to come here to talk about your spelling. Your examination is the worst example of a college student's spelling I've seen in five years of teaching.''

It was painful to listen as you showed me example after example of misspelled words that would have embarrassed a sixth-grader. ''Mr. Gentry, anyone as intelligent as you are who can't spell is lazy!''

You didn't lower my grade, for which I thank you. But as I walked out of your office I felt degraded nevertheless. I offered you no explanation for my poor spelling then. I submitted. But I knew I was not lazy about spelling.

In elementary school I had written two hundred and fifty-two perfect spelling tests. For thirty-six weeks each year, seven years in a row, I memorized the weekly spelling list so I could make 100 on the test. I was my school's expert at figuring out those inane exercises in the spelling textbook that require kids to dissect the most obscure properties of words imaginable — none of them remotely related to learning to spell. Even my teachers consulted me for help with those exercises. I always made A's in spelling, but I always knew I couldn't spell.

My grandmother knew. Not only could she spell well, she was a marvelous woman. For seven years she drilled me night after night on the weekly spelling list. "An A in spelling?" she would say with a twinkle in her eye when she looked at my report card.

Together, Grandma and I conspired to beat the system, to combat the subtle ignorances in spelling education, the absurdities of spelling grades, and the lunacy surrounding the focus on correct spelling. When I was in the seventh grade, she drilled and I memorized over 1600 words on a spelling list. I beat all the eighth-grade spellers in my school and took third place at the county spelling bee. By the time a write-up appeared in the local paper praising "the county's best spellers," I had forgotten about a quarter of the words on the list. "So you're one of the best spellers in the county," Grandma said as she read the article. We laughed.

Professor Henderson, I was *not* a lazy speller!

Your remarks that day in your office created a ripple. I now spend a lot of satisfying time and energy finding out more about how people learn to spell. I'm still not a good speller, but I now know why and I can accept the fact.

This book is dedicated to you, and to all teachers who misunderstand poor spellers. And to grandmothers, dads, friends, and teachers who help and support those of us who don't spell well.

Sincerely,
J. Richard Gentry, Ph.D.

Kneeling on rice

Teacher 1: How do *you* teach spelling?
Teacher 2: I've tried everything, every trick in the book. I use the basal
spelling series, work sheets, word copying, spelling bees, spelling
tests — there has to be a better way!

Fourteen elementary school teachers sat in a circle at a workshop talking about classroom practices that deter rather than promote spelling. Several confessed to red-penciling misspelled words on tests and lowering scores by a letter grade. Others made kids stay in at recess and write misspelled words twenty times. But Mrs. King stole the show. She remembered being ten years old in a parochial school where well-meaning teachers routinely punished kids for spelling errors. For missing five words in a fourth-grade composition, the nuns had made her kneel on rice! Her suggestion for improving spelling instruction was simple: "Please give kids soft rice!"

Why not! Spelling need not be surrounded by trauma. This book is about making spelling instruction more effective and learning to spell more natural.

Too much that is known about how to teach spelling isn't being put into practice. I can think of no subject we teach more poorly or harbor more myths about than spelling. In spite of volumes of research, teachers still use the same unsubstantiated teaching formulas. The spelling strategies and lessons you remember — whether you were in school one, two, or three generations ago — are still in use. Because of a conspiracy of ignorance, misunderstanding, and poor teaching methods, myths about spelling are lived out daily in thousands of classrooms. And parents may be bad spellers themselves, remembering only what school taught them — that bad spelling means bad kid.

It's time to separate fact from fiction, to replace mythology with reality. Some of the myths about spelling actually prevent normal spelling development. Yet they are widespread. They are considered part of our conventional wisdom. Parents and teachers should not spread them. Children should not be made their victims!

First let's examine the myths one by one, question their conventional wisdom, and indicate how or why each may interfere with the process of learning to spell.

- Spelling is serious business. Everyone must learn to spell.
- People who can't spell are ignorant.
- Spelling is supposed to be difficult.
- Spelling errors should not be tolerated.
- Good teachers reduce marks for poor spelling.
- Good spellers memorize a lot of information.
- Good spellers master a lot of rules.
- To become good spellers, kids have to do hundreds of spelling book exercises and drills.
- The most important thing about spelling is making 100% on spelling tests.
- Spelling is right or wrong. Good teachers always correct spelling.

Spelling is serious business. Everyone must learn to spell.

In reality, good spelling is merely a convenience. There are some people, like secretaries, who need to be accurate, but usually even they can use a word processor with a good spelling check. Those of us who spell poorly know we're competent in many other areas. Our weakness in spelling is okay. Not handy, but okay.

People who can't spell are ignorant.

There have been eminent scientists and brain surgeons, a famous president of Harvard University, and even presidents of the United States who couldn't spell. George Washington, Thomas Edison, and Auguste Rodin were atrocious spellers. Andrew Jackson, a pitiful speller, commented thus on intellect and spelling: "It's a damn poor mind that can think of only one way to spell a word!"

Spelling is supposed to be difficult.

Actually, some people find learning to spell easy and effortless. For others it may be a challenging task, partly because the system that has to be learned is complex. Spelling requires a complex mapping of form onto meaning. Expert spellers must have the knowledge and ability to honor certain conventions purely for the sake of correctness. In addition, learning to spell takes time.

On the positive side, children's early spelling, if invented in the context of writing, is both natural and predictable, and inventive spellers who spell spontaneously find spelling quite easy. This is not to suggest that learning to spell is incidental. Research indicates that we do need to teach formal spelling lessons to *supplement* what kids learn about spelling through reading and writing. But when we remove spelling from the context of writing, we make it more difficult. We should take care that our formal spelling lessons and our attitudes about spelling in children's writing are not arbitrary or capricious.

Consider the following quote from a teacher who thinks that spelling is supposed to be difficult:

> Spelling is very important. We shouldn't, as teachers, overlook misspelled words. In the long run, to do so will probably hurt the child. Make kids spell correctly. The only way they are going to learn to spell words they have trouble with is to *practice, practice, practice!*

This quote represents a popular but naive attitude toward spelling. Learning to spell may not be so difficult — nor teaching it so simple — as this teacher suggests. Perhaps she needs a more examined opinion of the process.

Spelling errors should not be tolerated.

One of the greatest difficulties a child can face in learning to spell is being inhibited from inventing spelling because of the risk of being wrong. Making errors is as natural for learning to spell as "ditching" is for learning to ride a bike. In both instances, learning cannot take place without error. Not only should spelling errors be tolerated, they should be expected. Very young children should be encouraged to invent their own spellings as a way of testing and modifying hypotheses about spelling. This is the way children learn.

Good teachers reduce marks for poor spelling.

Lowering grades for spelling places unnecessary physical and psychological constraints on writing. It makes writing a first draft hard, and besides, there is no evidence that reducing marks increases spelling competency. It's best to emphasize content in children's writing rather than correct spelling. The question of what fosters learning depends on the degree of emphasis, and content should receive the major, though of course not exclusive, emphasis. Good teachers teach proofreading skills and stress the value of correct spelling as well, but usually only for the final draft of a composition being readied for publication.

Good spellers memorize a lot of information.

Spelling is a complex cognitive process, not a simple memorization task. The visual memory required of the expert speller may be something good spellers are born with, not a skill one can consciously acquire. Many poor spellers simply can't memorize spellings and retain them.

Good spellers master a lot of rules.

Spelling is too complex to be memorized or learned by rules. Good spellers master a few rules that work consistently. Expert spellers rely heavily on tacit rules that work for them because they are already expert spellers.

To become good spellers, kids have to do hundreds of spelling book exercises and drills.

Ditto sheets, workbooks, and exercises don't create expert spellers. In fact, too much of what spelling workbooks require kids to do is not at all useful for learning to spell. Time spent on workbook exercises would generally be more valuable if the kids were allowed to do free writing and word study instead.

The most important thing about spelling is making 100% on spelling tests.

Teachers overemphasize the importance of spelling tests. Since spelling is not a simple memorization task, becoming a speller involves more than memorizing word lists. Research studies support the use of formal spelling instruction only if it consists of a systematic and logical program of word study that includes: introduction of a spelling vocabulary, phonics, prefixes, suffixes, word endings, compound words, homonyms, word origins, proofreading, and dictionary skills. Doing well on spelling tests alone will not ensure competency in spelling.

Spelling is right or wrong. Good teachers always correct spelling.

Good teachers are *not* touchy about minor points of spelling. In fact, undue emphasis on correct spelling often impedes children's spelling development. Anything that makes spelling unpleasant, more difficult, or threatening makes learning to spell more difficult. Children at the early stages of spelling development should not be expected to spell like adults. Keep in mind that language is learned as a constructive, developmental process. We expect a two-year-old to say "Daddy bye-bye," not "My father has departed." Likewise, we should expect a young speller 2 *Spel lik a chil not lik a ad dult.*

Let's give kids soft rice

Now let's replace those myths with reality.

- Some smart kids have trouble with spelling.
- Too much focus on "correctness" is bad for spelling.
- Copying words and focusing on mechanics don't ensure the development of correct spelling.
- Kids learn to spell by inventing spelling.
- Purposeful writing is a key to learning to spell.
- Spelling is a constructive developmental process.

Some smart kids have trouble with spelling.

Dan's mother sent her son to our Reading Center in January of his first-grade year. He was having difficulties with spelling. "I really don't like school," he complained, "and the worst thing about it is spelling."

Dan was a healthy, outgoing seven-year-old kid with straight blond hair that touched the collar of his faded sweatshirt. He propped his sneakers on the desk and his inquisitive blue eyes ricocheted about the room as I conducted the screening interview. After the first five minutes I wrote in my notebook "bright, active, articulate, inquisitive, uninhibited." Dan was positively garrulous when I asked him "What things do you like?" He talked about cars, sports, model airplanes, and collecting things. Then he emptied his pockets to show me some treasures garnered that day for his various collections: five coins, three stamps, a set of Dukes of Hazzard cards, and — what interested me most — a plastic sandwich bag carefully folded to protect a bluejay feather. Dan unfolded the bag, took out the feather, and twirled it between his thumb and forefinger as he discussed his feather collection. He already owned thirty-four feathers. He knew the species of each bird, and a good deal about each bird's habitat from the spot where he had found the feather. He was a smart and fascinating conversationalist.

I found out that books, pencils, pens, and paper had been at Dan's fingertips from babyhood. His home was a natural environment for written language. Both parents had an interest in reading and in ideas, and as early as three years of age, Dan could be seen toddling out of the public library hanging on to his mom with one hand and clutching *Green Eggs and Ham*, *Curious George Rides a Bike*, and *Dr. Seuss's ABC* in the other. He was read to every day. He was quick to read signs and labels by himself and readily understood what was read to him. "Dan has always liked books," his mother had noted in her application to the Reading Center.

I wasn't surprised to learn that Dan was an excellent student. By January he was reading above second-grade level. The problem was spelling. He fussed and fumed trying to decide which letters to choose. His parents encouraged him to write, but he said he hated spelling. He even complained when he tried to make lists of his collections and write notes for his own purposes.

On the day of our first meeting, I asked Dan how he felt about spelling. "It drives me crazy!" was his answer. At my request, he reluctantly produced the following story.

the Dukes of hazarD

the Sheriff always chases

Bo Duke and lukeDuke.

Many teachers would be pleased with this short piece from a first-grader. He remembered to indent for a paragraph and to end his sentence with a period. He chose a nice story line and his only errors were forgetting to capitalize and misspelling Hazzard. But I worried as I watched Dan write.

He pulled out his Dukes of Hazzard cards and looked at their labels. As he wrote the story, he shuffled through the cards to locate each word he needed. Then laboriously he copied the correct letters. He stopped and started over, drew a picture, and went to the water fountain twice — anything to avoid copying words. From the time he started, it took Dan forty-five minutes to produce the few words in his Dukes of Hazzard story. He was kneeling on very hard rice!

Too much focus on "correctness" is bad for spelling.

In his first six months of grade one, Dan had learned to expect failure at spelling. He had a good teacher in many respects, but she was vehement about correct spelling. By aggressively asserting that spelling is right or wrong, she had succeeded in making Dan feel helplessly anxious.

"My teacher says we have to spell it right!" Dan told me when I first asked him to invent a spelling. He already believed that spelling was difficult and tricky, and because he was not succeeding in pleasing his teacher, he was filled with dread.

His misplaced emphasis on correctness had begun in November with story copying. Dan and his friends had a "turkey story" lesson, a fairly typical primary-grade Thanksgiving assignment requiring them to copy a story written by the teacher. Even if the story had been imaginative, the instructions would have covered it up: "Now don't forget to indent for a paragraph. You must begin each sentence with a capital letter and end with the correct punctuation. I will count off for misspelling."

Twenty-six expressionless children did their seatwork, laboriously and grudgingly copying that turkey of a story for posting on a purple-backed bulletin board. Twenty-six sets of identical empty words, vacuous phrases, dead and barren sentences copied from the board. "Turkey stories" focus on correctness. And since they are composed by teachers, they take the ownership of beginning writing away from children.

I discovered what Dan thought the purpose of the exercise was: "To teach me to spell all the words right."

But copying correct spelling does little to enhance spelling ability. Spelling requires complex thinking. Copying is an exercise in eye-hand coordination requiring relatively simple mechanical ability and little brain power. Most kids find copying endless, mindless drudgery. When the emphasis is on correctness, it's also threatening. Mechanical copying activities make writing seem difficult and often make kids like Dan loathe spelling.

Copying words and focusing on mechanics don't ensure the development of correct spelling.

The "turkey story" pattern continued throughout Dan's first-grade year, leaving him very uptight. By January the children were spending hours copying the teacher's prefabricated stories. "Spell it right! You've got to spell it right!" was drilled into their heads. Some kids tried to "invent" spellings by choosing letters to match the sounds in the words. Papers were returned with red marks and x's. These marks spoke harshly: "You're wrong! If you can't spell it right, don't try it."

The kids learned. The "good" ones learned to put aside their own strategies. They submitted. When asked to write on their own, they made it short, using only words for which they had memorized spellings. Dan was quick to get the message: don't risk. Don't try to spell and nothing bad can happen to you. Spell and get it wrong and you're in trouble. So he played it safe. He copied and got it right. By January he refused to invent spellings. His only writing in school was copied from the chalkboard.

It was a big, big hill.   Dan
It was a big, big hill.
It was a big, big hill. This is beautiful!
It was a big, big hill.

Then, in April, the teacher announced that Dan should no longer copy, that he was old enough for "real" spelling. Unfortunately, at the same time she intensified her focus on mechanics. Dan's "Holden Beach" story came out of this phase.

We are going to the beach
and the name of are bea
ch is Holden beach![5]

Dan was drowning in a sea of correct spelling and mechanics. This is what he told me about his Holden Beach story:

Dan: In school today I had to spell. The teacher made me write this story but she helped me fix the words I couldn't spell. It took so long I couldn't stand it! If I didn't know a word, I had to go up to her desk and ask how to spell it. She wrote it on a paper and I came back to my desk to fix it. I had to get help on about eight words.

Gentry: What's this "fifteen" at the end of the first sentence?

Dan: Oh, she said I had to have fifty words so I counted them.

Dan was having to bow down to the god of mechanics. And kids don't become spellers by worshipping on a bed of hard rice!

Kids learn to spell by inventing spelling.

How I relived my own miserable spelling life as I worked with Dan! I desperately wanted to get him comfortable with spelling, so after the January interview I asked him to write another story. He continued the Dukes of Hazzard theme, laboriously copying three lines.

At that point I introduced him to the notion of inventing his own spellings. I had to really nudge to get him to try. Copying had given him no experience in segmenting the sounds of words, and he was almost paralyzed by his memories of school experiences in which he had tried to spell and got it wrong. Copying had merely given him a shield for self-protection. Dan was so confused and alienated by spelling that it seemed only a miracle of effort would be able to reclaim him. I literally had to pace him through the spelling of *sheriff*, sound by sound.

the Dukes
Bo Duke is John Schneider.
Luke Duke is Tom wopat.
they Jump ramps.
the shrff olwaz chass the Dukes.
the Dukes get away.
they have o cat named the Ginrl Lie

Dan: How do you spell *sheriff*?
Gentry: Try to spell it without my help.
Dan: But I can't spell it!
Gentry: (pronouncing the syllables) Sher-iff. Say the first part.
Dan: Sh. . .sh. . .
Gentry: Write that. (Dan writes *sh*)
Gentry: Sher-iff. What comes next?
Dan: (straining) Ruff. . .ruff.
Gentry: Write it. (Dan adds *r*)
Gentry: How does it end? (Dan writes *ff*)

This piece gives us a good opportunity to compare learning to spell by copying with learning by inventing.

Dan passively copied the correct spelling of *Schneider*, but that copying event was static and mechanical and Dan likely learned little about spelling in the process. Spelling is *not* a passive process. It is dynamic and complex. To learn to spell, Dan had to think. When he invented the spelling of *Ginrl Lie* in line six, he had to use what he already knew to fill his need to spell General Lee. His invented spelling was a synthesis of old and new knowledge. Learning occurred. Inventing *Ginrl Lie* required a deeper and more complex level of thinking than copying *Schneider*.

When kids invent spellings, they think about words and generate new knowledge. Emerging spellers need to invent, because inventing makes them think and learn.

Purposeful writing is a key to learning to spell.

Actually, inventing spelling and writing with a purpose are reciprocal ways to promote learning. When Dan began to invent spellings, he found it easier to write. As he wrote more and more, he learned more and more about writing. And purposeful writing, the writing Dan tried for audiences other than the teacher, helped him learn more about spelling. As he wrote, he invented spellings and engaged in thought about spelling, and his knowledge increased as he engaged in the process of spelling. Purposeful writing is an important key to learning to spell. It unlocks children's thinking about spelling by engaging them in the process.

Ironically, all that copying of "good" spelling in school had kept the doors to spelling closed for Dan. His school environment was hostile toward spelling. It had taught him that writing was difficult, that spelling was serious business, either right or wrong. The adult spelling his teacher insisted he use he found illogical and confusing. The copy work his teacher had him do was a monstrosity — painstaking, intensive, repetitive drudgery. It only succeeded in making him dislike writing and spelling altogether.

The next step for Dan was lots of practice with purposeful writing. "Dan," I said, "a magazine for teachers is publishing one of my articles about young children's writing. Could I use your stories in my article?" Dan liked the idea. It gave him a real purpose for writing. And I knew it would give him opportunities to invent many new spellings.

The idea of publishing spurred Dan into action. He was eager to write — at the Center, at home, everywhere except at school, where he still feared being punished for incorrect spelling. He added story after story to his growing collection. In all, he wrote thirty stories in sixteen weeks and invented one hundred and eighty-six spellings!

Here is a list of his titles:

The Dukes of Hazzard	*Out West*
The Dukes	*If I Had a Magic Pair of Boots*
Clifford	*States That I Have Been To*
My Oil Truck	*My Foot*
England	*The Circus*
The Mine	*Our Treehouse*
Muggs	*James Bond*
Toothpaste	*An Eagle*
My Coins	*Rocks*
The Toad	*$100.00*
Christmas	*If I Were a Pinball*
Outside	*My Grandmother*
Feelings	*My Dog*
Thanksgiving	*Blackout*
Halloween	*Lost*

Spelling is a constructive developmental process.

Dan's sixteen weeks at the Reading Center give us a dramatic record of children's spelling development. His writings show us the patterns and progression of early invented spellings. Learning to spell is like learning to speak: babbling, first words, two-word utterances, and later mature speech represent developmental stages in the constructive process of learning to speak. Spelling follows a similar pattern. It too begins with low-level strategies, followed by more complex productions as children self-correct and refine their language. Look for these characteristics as we examine the chronology of Dan's spelling at five developmental levels:

- development from simple to complex
- development from concrete to abstract representation
- self-correction
- refinement
- successive approximation of correct spelling

Dan's precommunicative spelling

Long before Dan went to school, as soon as he could hold a writing instrument, he engaged in pencil and paper activity and considered himself to be writing. He clearly liked this kind of activity. As all early writers do, he started out scribbling, but later he produced shapes that resembled letter forms. One of the first words he wrote was his name. By the time Dan was five, he could copy words and phrases he recognized (*I love you, 7-Up*), and he frequently filled page after page with letters of the alphabet. From these activities emerged precommunicative spelling, the earliest level of spelling development.

One day Dan's mom noticed him "spelling" in the car on the way to the grocery store. As they discussed what items they needed to buy, he reached under the seat, took out a crayon and pad his mom kept in the car for him, and began to write a grocery list, talking aloud as he did so.

Dan: This says 7-Up. (He writes.)
Dan: And we need milk. (He writes some more.)
Dan: Let's get some Raisin Bran and doughnuts. (He finishes the list.)

It is at the precommunicative spelling stage that kids first use alphabet symbols to represent words. When he made the grocery list, Dan wrote letters of the alphabet from memory, but he didn't know what sounds matched the letters. To form words in the grocery list, he strung letters together at random in the appropriate left-to-right fashion. At this stage his spelling attempts weren't readable because his letters didn't represent sounds. He was a spelling babbler.

Dan's semi-phonetic spelling

Dan's spelling was temporarily arrested in first grade, but it leapt forward again once he began to use invented spelling. He sped through four of the five developmental stages in a brief five-month period beginning in January. Normally these stages occur over two years, roughly between ages five and seven or eight. In the following sample, taken the first week in February, Dan wrote copiously about what he could do with magic. His thoughts ranged from fanciful illusions to negative feelings about school.

If I had a magic pair of boots, I would make gold. (24 crts).

I would blo' up the shoole.

I would play football.

I would read clfford books.

I would biy a camr.

I would blo up pluTo.

I would play baskball.

I would go to Newe york and see the stobu of lbrte

I would go out west.

I'd 'go to the grand canyn and biy a slatiti.

I would take d trip down the colordo rrevre on a raft.

Using a repetitive *I would. . .* pattern, Dan wrote more words than usual in this production and used both invented and "memorized" spellings. The memorized spellings don't tell us anything about what Dan knew at that time about spelling, but the misspellings (invented spellings) provide a window into his mind. The majority of Dan's misspelling's were *semi-phonetic.*

While he had advanced from the precommunicative stage to conceptualizing that letters represent the sounds in words, in fact Dan was lagging behind normal spelling for a bright seven-year-old who read at a second-grade level. After five months of first grade, he could only partially perceive and reliably represent the sounds in words. His semi-phonetic spelling was like telegraphic writing that omitted major sounds. He failed to map the complete sound structure of words to letters:

crts	carats	(omits ă)
camr	camera	(omits ə/ə)
baskball	basketball	(omits ĕt)
lbrte	liberty	(omits ĭ)
statiti	stalactite	(omits lăk)
colordo	Colorado	(omits ä)

Dan's phonetic spelling

As Dan increased his volume of writing, he continued to construct new spelling strategies and refine his invented spellings. By the first week in March he had clearly moved into the next developmental level.

my oll truck
My truck is gray.
My truck shuts water
out. on the side it ses
Mobol. It rais and Jumps ramps.
It's black) blue, red and
white. I Play weth it.

In "My Oil Truck," five of Dan's six invented spellings are phonetic. He had constructed a phonetic system of spelling that contained over eighty sound types, some reflecting obscure details of phonetic form. That's typically what phonetic spellers do. For the first time, he represented all of the surface sound features of words, and he systematically represented details of phonetic form for major speech sound categories: tense vowels, lax vowels, preconsonantal nasals, syllabic sonorants, inflectional endings, retroflex vowels, affricates, and intervocalic flaps.

Dan's basic spelling strategy at this stage was to spell the way it sounds. His relatively concrete mapping of letters to sounds was systematic, sophisticated, and perceptually accurate.

Dan's transitional spelling

The first Thursday in May, Dan came into the Reading Center, traced an outline of his foot on a piece of writing paper, and proceeded to write a lovely piece which he called "My Foot." He had reached the transitional spelling level.

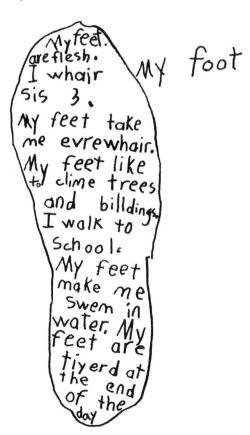

Notice his move from concrete to more abstract representation — one which required greater reliance on visual memory and less reliance on spelling words as they sound. Dan's spelling strategies now included spelling words as they look. By reading, writing, and thinking about spelling, he was developing a sense of when a particular spelling looked right. Given time and experience, this new visual strategy would become more fully developed.

What Dan knew about spelling at this stage included new knowledge about the conventions of English spelling. He put vowels in every syllable, used *e*-marker and vowel digraph patterns, spelled inflectional endings correctly, and used English letter sequences that occur frequently. Some of these conventions, not apparent in Dan's earlier samples, can be noted in the invented spellings in "My Foot."

whair	where	(digraph pattern and frequently occurring sequence)
clime	climb	(*e*-marker pattern)
billdings	buildings	(frequently occurring sequence)
tiyerd	tired	(digraph pattern and frequently occurring sequence)

Dan's mature spelling

Dan is now an accomplished correct speller. His mother came into the Reading Center last April, four years after his first-grade spelling program. She held in her hand a report of Dan's fifth-grade scores on the national achievement test, considered by many (certainly not by me!) to be the paragon of educational achievement. Compared with fifth-graders from across the nation, Dan had scored at the ninety-ninth percentile in spelling!

I suspect that the major cognitive changes necessary for spelling competency had been accomplished by the time Dan was eight years old. He had become comfortable with spelling by the end of grade one and no longer needed sessions at the Center. Beginning in grade two, he began to achieve success in formal spelling instruction. He continued to learn, from being attentive to and interested in spelling through writing experiences. Now spelling well above grade level, what Dan had learned about spelling matched the characteristics of the developmentally correct speller.

- He understood the English spelling system and its basic rules.

- He had mastered accurate spelling of prefixes, suffixes, contractions, compound words.

- He knew how to distinguish homonyms.

- He usually used silent letters and double consonants correctly.

- When spelling a new word, he could think of alternative spellings and visualize the word in his mind's eye.

- He had mastered many irregular spellings.

- He was beginning to recognize word origins and to use this information to make meaningful associations.

- He was accumulating a large corpus of known spellings.

I expressed my great pleasure at Dan's success as a speller. His mother was smiling. She pulled out a card that Dan had written to his granny the night before the national achievement test.

My picture

Thanks, for giving me the $5 dollars I really aprisiate it. I have to admit it was a good picture. I hope I can visit soon or you come over. Well I gotta go.
Love,
Dan

"Appreciate" was spelled *aprisiate*. Dan, one of the best fifth-grade spellers in the nation, was still inventing spelling!

Not all children will learn to spell well.

I have a Ph.D. in spelling. I still suffer from poor-speller's anxiety. In writing the first third of this book, I made forty-seven spelling errors in the rough draft. I corrected thirty-five and my proofreaders corrected the other twelve. Good spelling is at best a convenience. Nonetheless, I do know that there are crucial times when the words I write must be correctly spelled. I own thirteen dictionaries and use them constantly:

The American Heritage Dictionary (new college edition)
A Dictionary of Reading and Related Terms
The Elementary Spelling Book (an improvement on *The American Spelling Book* by Noah Webster)
The New York Times Everyday Dictionary
The Random House Dictionary (two editions)
Scholastic Dictionary of Synonyms, Antonyms, Homonyms
Webster's New Collegiate Dictionary
Webster's New Twentieth Century Dictionary (Second edition, unabridged)
Webster's New World Dictionary of the American Language (four different editions)

I get additional help from my secretary (a good speller), from colleagues who read my work and correct my misspellings, and from the spelling check in my word processor.

My research on spelling over the past twelve years has exposed me to studies of human cognition, linguistics, child development, and behavioral science, all of which offer insights on the spelling process and on how we learn to spell. Although I've learned much about teaching and coaching children to spell, I've made little progress, after twelve years of study, in bettering *myself* as a speller.

I now understand that expert spellers develop a memory capacity for visual images of words. I simply do not have a completely functioning visual coding mechanism for spelling. Many spellers don't. We aren't lazy, as Professor Henderson suggested, but without that capacity, we *are* poor spellers. Researchers need to learn more about the visual coding mechanism for spelling — perhaps some instructional activity will help children acquire it.

Questions teachers ask

Spelling is one of the most widely researched areas of the language arts, and systematic studies are providing answers to some of the questions teachers ask. In my view, the important questions center on an understanding of how children learn, and the important answers place children, not methods, at the center of the spelling program. But teachers also express very practical concerns about methods and teaching strategies, about how best to proceed with the formal spelling study that research agrees is necessary.

- What method for teaching spelling works best?
- What teaching strategies will help create an effective program?
- For our spelling lessons, what procedures can we use that are supported by research?
- What is the single best strategy for a formal spelling lesson?
- Shouldn't invented spelling be corrected? If errors aren't corrected, won't misspellings become habitual?
- When should formal spelling instruction begin?
- What spelling rules should be taught?
- Who chooses the words in spelling books? How do they choose?
- What is the best way to help children learn how to spell the words they miss on spelling tests?
- Should phonics be taught as a basis for spelling?

What method for teaching spelling works best?

Allowing children the freedom to take risks in their own writing is the best technique I know of. Children learn to speak by speaking, making mistakes and refining their language as they communicate. So they learn how to spell by writing, inventing spellings, and refining their understanding of print. The process involves active participation and risk-taking. Both writing and risk-taking provide important opportunities for learning to spell. Children need a supportive environment that stimulates their interest and enthusiasm for self-expression through writing. They need freedom to test and modify their hypotheses about spelling.

To teach kids to spell, get them to write. Break down the inhibitions and unpleasantness surrounding spelling and allow kids the chance to be wrong. This technique isn't simple. Nor does it suggest that spelling is learned exclusively in an informal manner — that is, incidentally through children's experiences in writing. But taking risks does provide critical opportunities for learning to spell.

Remember Dan's experiences in first grade. If the cost of mistakes is too high, children cease taking risks and are likely to have difficulty learning to spell.

What teaching strategies will help create an effective program?

Teacher: I've been teaching for eleven years but I've never found very good strategies for teaching spelling.

There are five general guidelines for creating an effective spelling program:

- Teach spelling as part of the whole curriculum. Capitalize on opportunities to have children write and spell in situations other than the spelling lesson — in math, history, and science lessons, for instance.

- Have children write frequently. Children invent and refine spelling using the skills they acquire when they write. Spelling practice occurs through free writing, when children write labels, lists, signs, plans, stories, songs, recipes, and letters. Remember to make the writing activity purposeful.

- *Encourage* children to invent spellings for words they may not have learned to spell. Inventing spellings allows children to engage in thinking about words and to demonstrate their acquired skills.

- De-emphasize correctness, memorization, and writing mechanics. Adjust your expectations for correctness to fit the children's level of development and make allowances for inexperience and mistakes.

- Respond to children's writing in ways that help them discover more about spelling. In your response, build interest in words, make word study fun, answer questions about spelling, and teach spelling skills. Help young writers develop a positive spelling consciousness.

For our spelling lessons, what procedures can we use that are supported by research?

I'm always happy when teachers ask what instructional strategies for teaching spelling are supported by research. Those who ask have an easier time getting rid of the myths I talked about at the beginning.

In the context of formal spelling instruction, there are six procedures that receive research support:

- Allot sixty to seventy-five minutes per week to formal spelling instruction.

- Present the words to be studied in list or column form.

- Give the children a pre-test to determine which words in the lesson are unknown. Have them study the unknown words, then administer a post-test.

- Have the children correct their own spelling tests under your direction.

- Teach a systematic technique for studying unknown words.

- Use spelling games to make spelling lessons more fun.

What is the single best strategy for a formal spelling lesson?

I don't think there is one! What works best for one child may not work well for another. One technique frequently cited as being most effective is this: have children correct their own spelling errors immediately after taking a spelling test. Often the teacher spells the word orally for the children to check, or provides the correct written model. Or corrections are made during conferences, in response to questions from the children. This technique is effective because it gets children to examine their spelling errors visually. Expert spellers develop a visual memory for words. Although we can't define visual memory, we know it is complex and largely hidden from conscious awareness. Having kids correct their own errors immediately seems to aid their visual memory.

Shouldn't invented spelling be corrected? If errors aren't corrected won't misspellings become habitual?

Errors shouldn't be corrected to the extent that children are afraid to spell. Beginning spellers should be absolutely free to invent spellings when they write. There is no evidence that invented spellings become habitual. Of course poor spellers habitually misspell certain words. But children who are encouraged to invent spellings will refine those spellings and progress developmentally toward correctness. It is perfectly acceptable to publish or display young childrens' invented spelling without correcting it.

As a speller matures, emphasis on correctness should increase. Still, it's best to hold children absolutely accountable for correct spelling only in the context of final drafts of compositions being readied for publication. For a grocery list, it really doesn't matter if the word written is *katchup, catchup,* or *ketchup.*

When should formal spelling instruction begin?

Consider the following vignettes:

Scott's first-grade teacher notes in a writing conference that he is using the common phonetic strategy of spelling *lat* for *let*. She understands the logic of this choice — he has probably noted that ĕ (the short vowel sound in *let*) sounds more like the letter-name *a* than like *e, i, o,* or *u*. In conference, she points out the actual spelling of *let* and gives him five other words from his writing to illustrate the short *e* sound. He learns to spell these words before the next writing conference. Scott's teacher is teaching a formal spelling lesson. At the same time, she doesn't deny the validity of Scott's categorization. She knows his use of *a* for the ĕ sound doesn't indicate that something is wrong with his hearing. Her objective is to add to what he knows by providing the standard spelling for the sound in question while recognizing the integrity of his letter-name strategy, which works for him in other contexts.

Jennifer writes *duc* for *duck*. Although she knows that *c* represents *k* in some positions, she hasn't yet generalized the rule for *-k* in the final position. Her teacher knows that Jennifer can recognize some words that end in *-ck* when she reads. She even spells some *-ck* words correctly. But knowing those final *-ck* spellings has not changed her judgment about the spelling for *duck*. The teacher selects *duck* for study and shows Jennifer how to classify it with the other words she knows that have *-ck* in the final position. Again the teacher is involved in formal spelling instruction.

Laura loves writing letters. She also keeps a journal which she freely shows her teacher. The teacher makes it a point to respond in writing to Laura's comments, sometimes by asking a question that will elicit further writing. Laura's responses incorporate both the conventional spellings of the words her teacher uses and invented spellings of her own. Even in modeling conventional spellings in this way, Laura's teacher is providing a form of spelling instruction.

These vignettes illustrate how instruction in spelling may spring from both formal and informal interactions with very young children when they write. With frequent writing, many of the errors that arise when children make use of their limited spelling knowledge will disappear. Instances such as the first two, where the teacher intervened while Scott and Jennifer were constructing invented spellings, capture the optimal moments when teaching can extend children's knowledge and experience with spelling.

Individualizing spelling instruction should continue as kids arrive at readiness for studying word lists and participating in more formalized spelling lessons. Traditionally, formal spelling instruction begins in the second grade, a practice that fits with what we know about developmental spelling. By second grade, many children spell at the phonetic and transitional developmental levels and do profit from formal study. But children at lower developmental levels may experience frustration if they are pushed too soon into formal spelling. For best results, individualize and use small groups for formal spelling instruction. Allow writing conferences to guide you in determining when kids are ready for formalized instruction.

What spelling rules should be taught?

Spelling is much too complex to be learned by memorizing rules. Teach only the rules that apply to a large number of words, not those that have lots of exceptions. There are only a few good spelling rules that need to be taught:

- the rules for using periods in abbreviations
- the rules for using apostrophes to show possession
- the rules for capitalizing proper names and adjectives
- the rules for adding suffixes (changing *y* to *i*, dropping the final silent *e*, doubling the final consonant)
- the rule that English words don't end in *v*
- the rule that *q* is followed by *u* in English spelling

Who chooses the words in spelling books? How do they choose?

Publishing companies use different formulas and word lists for selecting the words that go into particular spelling series. Most often, words are selected based on the following criteria:

- frequency of use in children's writing
- frequency of use in children's oral vocabulary
- degree of difficulty
- universality and permanency in our language
- application to other academic subjects

Often the words in a series are organized into lessons to demonstrate specific phonetic or structural generalizations. The publishing company or series author usually draws words from several published lists, including the following:

American Heritage Words Frequency Book
Teaching Spelling: Canadian Word List and Instructional Techniques
Basic Elementary Reading Vocabulary

The Living Word Vocabulary
The New Iowa Spelling Scale
Phoneme Grapheme Correspondences as Cues to Spelling Improvement

Most spelling series introduce about 3000 words, which account for 97% of all the words children use in their writing.

What is the best way to help children learn how to spell the words they miss on spelling tests?

You should provide guidelines for effective word study techniques. For most children, effective methods for studying unknown words would include visual inspection, auditory inspection, kinesthetic reinforcement, and recall — always with the words treated as wholes. Here are two examples of effective techniques:

Fitzgerald method (1951)
1. Look at the word carefully.
2. Say the word.
3. With eyes closed, visualize the word.
4. Cover the word and then write it.
5. Check the spelling.
6. If the word is misspelled, repeat steps 1-5.

Horn method (1954)
1. Pronounce each word carefully.
2. Look carefully at each part of the word as you say it.
3. Say the letters in sequence.
4. Attempt to recall how the word looks, then spell it.
5. Check this attempt to recall.
6. Write the word.
7. Check this spelling attempt.
8. Repeat the above steps if necessary.

Simply writing the words in question a certain number of times is *not* a good procedure for learning misspelled words.

Should phonics be taught as a basis for spelling?

Should you teach phonics (speech sounds and their spelling correspondences) to help children learn to spell? There is no easy or irrefutable answer to this question, although we do know that phonics instruction does not result in error-free spelling. A well-known study of phonics rules and spelling is often cited by both those who object to and those who advocate phonics instruction. According to that study, knowledge of phonics enables a person to spell only one of every two words. Stated another way, the study shows that by using phonics rules a person can write 87% of common words with a maximum of one error per word.

Is phonics a necessary but insufficient technique? Evidence seems to indicate that phonics instruction does help spelling achievement. At least it provides an effective scheme for organizing word lists in the spelling series used in early elementary grades. But words studied formally should also be considered for frequency and meaning. Direct, systematic teaching of word study, including phonics, should supplement learning to spell through reading and writing, but it should be kept in proper perspective. Formal spelling study should be limited to about seventy-five minutes per week. The real foundation for spelling is frequent writing.

Advice for parents

Parents are important spelling teachers who play an active role in shaping their children's attitudes about spelling. Some parents just naturally seem to do what is right, helpful, and supportive for their children's rapid development. But all parents can learn from teachers. Good parent education is an important component of a quality spelling program.

Reading and writing in the home contribute to children's academic development throughout the preschool, as well as the school-age years. Some parents intuitively provide an environment that enhances literacy development. They share books, read to their children, and encourage them to scribble, draw, and write. These activities are not only fun, they are important in the children's educational development. Reading books, storytelling, story listening, scribbling, and writing are the important first steps to literacy. Let me give you an example.

Ann Edwards and her husband Don have an intuitive understanding of what parents should do in the home to teach reading, writing, and spelling. Even though Ann is a teacher, she never thought of their daughter Meredith's enthusiastic preschool involvement with print as "teaching." According to Ann, "For Meredith, Don and me, writing and spelling have always been just for fun." Meredith has never known a world without books, and paper, and writing. She scribbled messages on greeting cards before she was two years old, spelled her name when she was four, and wrote stories by the time she was five. Her spelling competency developed from living in a world of print with parents who encouraged her to satisfy her natural curiosity.

Meredith learned to spell by trying to make sense of the print in her environment, most of which was provided by parents who took joy in sharing that print with their child. Books, greeting cards, magazines, newspapers, notes, scribbling, letters, words — all were ever-present sources of fun and fascination. Their explorations with her were purposeful, genuine, and unrelated to conscious efforts to teach. Unfortunately, not all children are fortunate enough to have parents who encourage such print-related activities in the home. Often teachers must be parent educators as well, providing parents with suggestions and guidance for participation in their children's literacy development.

The six samples that follow, written by Meredith at various times from two to six years of age, show her growing knowledge of spelling, without schooling or formal exposure to teaching.

Scribbled message on a greeting card (2 years, 4 months)

Scribbling and spelling on a greeting card (3 years, 5 months)

If these wishes
for your birthday
Will every one come true,
Then the nicest grandmother
in the world
Will be the happiest, too!

HAPPY BIRTHDAY!

M ETEOI

Spelling of her name (4 years, 3 months)

DNe
peNrdre

Story describing a picture of her father (5 years)

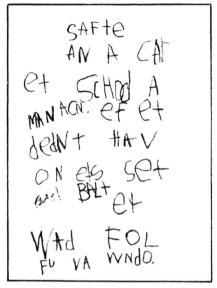

SAFte
AN A CAt
et SCHod A
MAN ACN. ef et
dedN+ HAV
ON es Set
and BALt et
WAd FOL
Fu VA WNdO.

Story describing a film that had mannequins
wearing seatbelts (5 years, 3 months)

My Babe store

I was baon on
Janurre the 4. I
Git baon At 5-0-lo
I Waod Arad 1 PAnd.
ThE farst time I
And at had ABCs
oN at . I ate ham
Ahd Grren Beas meat.
Meredith Ann
Edwards
weat to Weastn saLn
I dead a stexee in
my Moms Lap. I
War a wiet. drgs
Neth Las oN eat,

Autobiographical sketch (6 years, 5 months)

Let's have a look at some guidelines for educating parents.

- Show parents that spelling is a developmental process.
- Let parents know that writing is important.
- Advise parents not to be critical.
- Introduce parents to the concept of invented spelling.
- Persuade parents to make time for writing.
- Encourage parents to have fun with spelling.

Show parents that spelling is a developmental process.

Much of this book is devoted to helping teachers understand that spelling is a developmental process. Parents can reach the same understanding if you show them that learning to spell unfolds over time, like learning to speak. Parents typically view spelling as rote memorization. Many remember their own spelling books, with lists of words to be memorized. They think of spelling as something to be assigned, tested, and graded.

But kids don't learn to spell by memorizing word lists. The process is much more complex. To learn to represent language in visual form by use of graphic symbols, kids must experience ongoing interactions with written language over time. They must explore the patterns that form English spelling and develop an understanding of its complex structure. They must have experiences with printed language that lead from a simple to a complex understanding of English spelling. These experiences allow them to construct their knowledge of the spelling system. Showing parents samples of children's writing at various developmental stages, and pointing out the changes that are taking place, will help them understand the developmental nature of learning to spell.

Let parents know that writing is important.

You can help parents recognize the importance of writing. To become better spellers, kids must do lots of writing. After all, the only reason kids learn to spell to begin with is so they can write. Writing allows them to add new words to their spelling repertoire and engages their thinking about spelling. In addition, writing at home gets kids to use their acquired spelling knowledge. It exercises their spelling skills and keeps them from getting rusty as spellers. Kids who don't write suffer from spelling disuse.

Tell parents not to worry about correcting misspelling on their kids' papers. The evidence is clear that kids who write frequently, even those who receive no spelling corrections, become better writers — in fact, they may make even *fewer* spelling errors than those who receive corrections. Always urge parents to encourage their kids to write. The kids have so much to gain!

Advise parents not to be critical.

Tell parents that when their children write at home they should reserve their comments for the content of the writing and not be critical of spelling errors. They should react to the children's *ideas,* accompanying their comments with praise and encouragement for the writing. In general parents should not correct their children's papers — corrections are usually construed as criticism.

A parent seeing seven-year-old Steven's story about snakes might feel compelled to be critical of his spelling:

Today were gowing to talk about snaycks. A snayck is a anumml that slithers ~~es~~ and can be dayjris and can be puysunis. Sum ar not. It can sqkwes you if you bot it. Cefl. You can be in dayjre by a snayck.
the in

Consider the following response from his mother:

> Steven, I like the story but you don't know how to spell. You misspelled *animal, today, going, talk, about, snakes, dangerous, poisonous, some, are, squeeze, bother, careful, danger* and *end*. I'll correct them so you can rewrite the story with the right spelling.

It's unlikely that Steven would volunteer to write more stories after this kind of response. If he did, he'd likely ask an adult for the correct spelling, or use only spellings he had memorized. Neither of these options would challenge Steven to think about spelling.

His mother's comments should focus on the story's content. She should praise his spelling attempts, which were good for a seven-year-old, and ask him which words he had difficulty spelling. It would be fine for her to produce a copy of the story with correct spellings, keeping in mind that Steven is not at a level of readiness to spell all of the words. The value of presenting him with a corrected version would be to heighten his spelling consciousness and provide an early model of proofreading and revision. Since spelling development is influenced by seeing standard spelling, there might be some value in exposing Steven to the correct visual representation of the words. But at this level, seeing corrected spellings, or even copying the story with corrected spellings, wouldn't enable Steven to add these words to his spelling repertoire. Correct spelling for most of them will come later in his development.

Steven's composition about snakes is a fine story. There is little to be gained from criticizing it.

Introduce parents to the concept of invented spelling.

Parents who have listened to their children babble, speak their first words, and eventually advance to mature speech have seen language develop as a constructive process over time. Pointing out to them the importance of babbling for eventual speech competency will help them understand the importance of hypothesizing and testing ideas about spelling for eventual spelling competency. When young children like Steven use what they know about the spelling system to guess a word's spelling, parents should realize that they are "inventing" spelling, not just spelling incorrectly. Inventing spelling is a thinking process. It may begin as early as three or four years of age. First children learn to recognize some of the letters of the alphabet and to name them by their names. Then they use letters to spell sounds, often the sounds heard in the letter-names: for instance, *n* spells *in*. This insight is extended so letters are used to spell messages, and a spelling system has been invented. Invented spellings are everyday occurrences in young children's writing.

Children move through developmental stages of invented spelling as they move through developmental stages of speech. Parents should understand that invented spelling doesn't lead to the formation of bad spelling habits. When children encounter new information about standard spelling, they readily modify their hypotheses and have no difficulty adopting standard spelling. Ultimately, the expert speller is able to use information from visual memory, as well as knowledge of phonetic, contextual, and meaning relationships to determine the correct spelling of a word. But the process takes time. Important foundations of learning to spell are set with the use of invented spelling.

Persuade parents to make time for writing.

According to some recent statistics, the average child who finishes kindergarten has already watched more than 5000 hours of television — more time than it takes a college student to earn a bachelor's degree. There are times when the television should be turned off so kids can pursue other activities, like writing. Making time for writing includes engaging in family writing activities: the family writes together and shares its writing. Watching their parents write can be a great incentive for children to write themselves. Sharing family writing — letters to loved ones, accounts of special family events, family histories, trip journals, story writing, lists for camping trips — can be fun. Motivation for children's writing in the home should come from the fun or utility of the writing, not from force. A starting point is to remind parents to cut out some of the competing activities and set aside time for writing.

Encourage parents to have fun with spelling.

Too often, when parents get involved, kids have little or no fun with spelling. There are many ways that parents can make spelling fun. One of the best ways of promoting interest and enthusiasm is through spelling games. These can be simple "made up" games for playing on long trips in the family car — for instance, "I spy something that begins with *A*" and "hangman" — or electronic ones such as *Speak and Spell*, spelling games for the home computer, board games such as *Scrabble* and *Wheel of Fortune*, and commercial ones such as *Probe* or *Spill and Spell*. Remind parents that spelling in the home should extend beyond those frustrating Thursday night efforts to force children to memorize a list of words for the test on Friday. Spelling should be fun!

Is *spel*. . . a four-letter word?

Must spelling be taught in a way offensive to children? How I hated spelling! Week after week I battered my brains against formidable bastions of word lists, rules, exercises, definitions, phonics, and sentence dictations. I submitted to my teachers' plans for making me a perfect speller. I enjoyed small successes along the way — gold stars, some good grades — but I knew that most of my hard work was in vain. I wasn't learning to spell very well, and I experienced the pain of others pointing this out to me without doing anything to help.

In elementary school I collected memorabilia. Samples of my early writing dutifully pasted in a scrapbook document the presence of an emerging spelling enigma: I worked hard, but I wasn't getting the results. Here is one sample from a 4-H livestock record book I kept in fifth grade. It's a perfect demonstration of my poorly developing visual coding mechanism. Notice my spelling of *selected* right after the word *select*.

Summary

1. Why did you select this project? *I sollected a steer becase I thought it would be a good 4 H project.*

The final draft of my narrative report on "My 4-H Steer" is equally revealing. Painstakingly copied in ink, and no doubt proofread more sedulously than is usual for a ten-year-old, it is filled with errors that suggest a poor memory capacity for visual images of words. When I proofread I didn't "see" errors that would have been obvious to most proofreaders:

the	for	*they*
to	for	*too*
ben	for	*been*
befor	for	*before*
weighted	for	*weighed*
whild	for	*while*
ribons	for	*ribbons*
stoped	for	*stopped*

My 4-H Steer

My daddy sold me my calf. My brother had a calf with mine. We kept them in a pen and fed them every morning and night. At first my calf was wild. As we worked with them the became tame.

In the winter it was to cold to wash him. When it got warm he was not as tame as he had ben. He would run away every time I got him out, but after several weeks of work I had him tame.

A few days before time to take him to Durham Mr. Smith came out to the house to help me shear my calf. The next day we washed them up and got them ready for the show.

When we got to Durham we had to wait to get him weighed While I was waiting a man took my picture with my steer and put it in the newspaper.

Fri. night we had the showing. They gave out the Blue ribons and then the red ribons and came down to me and stoped! Oh I wanted one so bad. But that was that.

Sat. night we sold them and then came the worst time of all leaving my colf! But I had made a good profit and was happy.

Richard Gentry

The chart below provides a publishing history of each word I misspelled. Six of the eight would have appeared in my spelling books *before* grade five. It's likely I had spelled both *ribbon* and *stopped* on weekly tests before I wrote the report at the end of my fifth-grade year.

Publishing History of Eight Spelling Words

Word	they	too	been	before	weight	while	ribbon	stopped
Mean grade level for presentation in a spelling series	2.04	3.23	2.56	3.36	5.45	3.26	4.87	3.91
Grade level at which the word is most often taught	1	2	2	2	5	2	5	5
How many of 20 publishers include the word	15	17	14	15	15	16	13	11
Included in how many of 20 high-frequency word lists	20	20	19	20	11	16	9	15

There is no way I could have escaped those words on my successful weekly spelling tests!

It should have been obvious that I was having special difficulties with spelling. I worked so hard. I mastered every weekly list. And yet my writing was full of inaccuracies. I have no recollection of any sympathetic teacher ever working with me individually on my problems. It would have been easy to analyze a few of my writing samples and help me with the major problem areas so apparent in my 4-H report: I needed to review and learn certain high-frequency homonyms, to be shown how double consonants mark syllable divisions, to be reinstructed in certain basic rules I didn't understand about inflectional endings. My teachers may not have been able to rectify the limitations of my visual memory, but they certainly might have addressed a few problem areas that would have enhanced my spelling accuracy and made my spelling disability more palatable.

And things haven't changed much since I was in school. Spelling curriculum is dished out like fast-food burgers: ketchup, mustard, pickle — no substitutions. I was fed the same precooked spelling curriculum that all kids get in elementary school, with no attention paid to individual problems, needs, or desires. Even today it's mostly mush for memory from a plate of ready-made curriculum.

Evaluation and assessment are equally problematic. It's true that I always made 100's on the weekly spelling tests. But my report cards revealed my teachers' whimsical grading — both my best grade ever (A) and my worst ever (B-) were in spelling!

Maybe some teachers based grades on effort, some on weekly spelling tests, and others on demonstrated competence. I only remember being confused and not getting any help. The teachers who lowered my grades because of poor spelling offered no special instruction. Their obligation seemed to stop at pointing out my weaknesses. There's got to be more to teaching than that!

I believe that teachers and parents have created a fundamental opposition between children and the spelling curriculum. Children are ignored in favor of teaching fixed and ready-made sets of facts and formulas. This tension is inappropriate if our objective is to get kids to learn to spell. It has created a set of false dichotomies that prejudice children against spelling.

Spelling	vs	*Children*
right	vs	wrong
standard	vs	non-standard

good	vs	bad
discipline	vs	laziness
order	vs	chaos
convention	vs	anarchy
success	vs	failure
praise	vs	embarrassment

Unconsciously we cause children to associate spelling with being wrong, non-standard, bad. We accuse bad spellers of being lazy. We cause chaos in composition, anarchy in learning. A spelling-first curriculum often leads to failure and embarrassment. And we have a very long record of having put spelling at the center of the curriculum without seeing widespread competency.

If the curriculum-first program had worked, by all accounts I *should* have become an excellent speller. But try as I might, I never learned how to spell well. Instead, I developed undesirable attitudes and emotions. As open and willing as I was to having my teachers pour their spelling knowledge into my brain, it never happened.

I suspect the problem was, and is for many children, that learning doesn't begin with a subject. Learning begins and takes place in an individual child's mind. John Dewey knew that when he suggested that we start with a child's mind and allow learning to move outward. It's time for parents and teachers to learn from Dewey, who described a curriculum-centered discipline this way:

> Subdivide each topic into studies; each study into lessons; each lesson into specific facts and formulae. Let the child proceed step by step to master each of these separate parts, and at last he will have covered the entire ground. The road, which looks so long when viewed in its entirety, is easily traveled, considered as a series of particular steps. Thus emphasis is put upon the logical subdivisions and consecutions of the subject-matter. Problems of instruction are problems of procuring texts giving logical parts and sequences, and of presenting these portions in class in a similar definite and graded way. Subject-matter furnishes the end, and it determines method. The child is simply the immature being who is to be matured; he is the superficial being who is to be deepened; his is narrow experience which is to be widened. It is his to receive, to accept. His part is fulfilled when he is ductile and docile.

A spelling curriculum that requires seven or eight years of memorizing word lists and remembering isolated facts is not likely to "deepen" children. A few kids who have good visual memories for words will find word lists easy. They'll be successful with little effort. Not surprisingly, these kids may like spelling. But for most children, spelling presented as "stuff" for memory becomes dead symbols with no bridge between the facts and their experiences.

When spelling is *not* taught socially in interaction with reading, writing, and other language arts, most kids will see no purpose or use for it. They won't like it, nor will they be motivated to master it. For these kids, a ready-made spelling curriculum not related to their personal experience is boring. In this context, many will not learn to spell.

I think the alternative is straightforward: *put children first when teaching spelling*. Make spelling a child-centered discipline. John Dewey also described how spelling can be taught in a child-centered curriculum:

> The child is the starting-point, the center, and the end. His development, his growth, is the ideal. It alone furnishes the standard. To the growth of the child all studies are subservient; they are instruments valued as they serve the needs of growth. Personality, character, is more than subject-matter. Not knowledge or information, but self-realization, is the goal. To possess all the world of knowledge and lose one's own self is as awful a fate in education as in religion. Moreover, subject-matter never can be got into the child from without. Learning is active. It involves reaching out of the mind. It involves organic assimilation starting from within. Literally, we must take our stand with the child and our departure from him. It is he and not the subject-matter which determines both quality and quantity of learning.

You know, I *like* spelling in this context. Now *spell* is no longer a four-letter word!

I've described spelling as a constructive, developmental process. Meredith and Dan became actively involved with learning to spell when spelling became part of their social setting. They sent messages on greeting cards and published stories in a magazine. They wanted to spell. They tried to spell. Then they learned through a process of continuous reconstruction that took place in their minds.

Learning to spell is organic when it grows outward from children's present experience. It is social when it is done to share information with others, or when it evokes a desired response from someone else. Once we accept children as the center of the spelling curriculum, what's left is to discover the steps — organic, social, and instructional — that nurture their growth from their present experience to a richer maturity.

Teaching spelling should follow the rich new findings of the other language arts. There must be freedom to take risks, freedom to be wrong, freedom to take command. There has to be room for individual differences, for discovery, experimentation, and choices. There has to be acceptance of the fact that some of us will never spell as well as others. We need that understanding. It is not necessary for all people to sing equally well, paint landscapes, drive racing cars, do calculus, play the cello, teach, or spell equally well. They simply become the best they can.

What I've discovered, and what I've tried to demonstrate in this book, is that by placing children at the center of the curriculum we can teach spelling in a natural way that eliminates pain, disappointment, and failure. Children can learn how to spell in the same organic, developmental way they learn how to speak. Formal instruction can help, but always in a social context. Spelling can be presented as a powerful gift of literacy passed on by elders. It can be taught by having children do it, not by having it done to them.

John Dewey's insights have been supported by the research of the last several decades. We now have convincing evidence that:

● Learning to spell is an organic, developmental process.

● Learning to spell is a conceptual process. It involves thinking, not rote memorization.

● Spelling should be taught socially in interaction with reading, writing, and the other language arts — and with people.

● Formal spelling programs should not focus on tedious drills with irksome materials and hideous tests, but should take place in a context that honors the recent understandings of children's developing orthographic knowledge, principles that can be applied in a child-centered curriculum.

Spelling should be taught as a human right, not as a human obligation. We must free children to learn to spell.

Postscript: Pain prevention

I still feel the pain of my childhood problems with spelling. I shall never forget my painful meeting with Dr. Henderson. In a way, my professional life has been an attempt to lessen my own pain and prevent the same kind of pain for children now in school. I would like to reach all those who figure large in the learning lives of children and ask them to benefit from my (and possibly their own) experiences. So I've written three letters. Two of them are appeals to the adults responsible for spelling programs in the schools. The other is a reassuring note to children. Will you help me reach the addressees?

Dear School Board Members and Administrators,

I would like to propose a better way to teach spelling. It doesn't call for extensive curriculum changes or elaborate increases in budget. You can't buy it from a catalogue or get a curriculum committee to design it. It has simply grown up from a newfound belief in the value of children's writing: if children are allowed to develop as writers, and if teachers watch them and help them, spelling <u>will</u> improve.

I've always been a bad speller, and I hated spelling lessons. They never did me any good. In the last few decades research has discovered that:

-- Children should enjoy spelling.

-- Children should feel free to use spelling as a tool for writing and learning.

-- The spelling curriculum should allow children to realize their full potential, not only as spellers, but also as writers.

If my own teachers had known those things, I think they would not have made me spend so many hours preparing for weekly spelling tests (which I passed without ever becoming a better speller). Rather, they would have:

-- Let me write a lot. Spellers need to write. Daily purposeful writing in and out of the classroom enhances spelling. Spelling competency grows with application through writing.

-- Let me try out spellings. Spellers need to take risks. Children learn to spell the same way they learn to speak, not through memorization, but by conceptualizing a complex process. Spellers must use spelling. We should worry less about correcting bad spelling and more about encouraging children to try out their own spellings.

-- Been more aware of my problems with spelling. When spelling is taught directly, we should teach the children, not the materials. We need to make spelling a child-centered curriculum. We need to select materials and techniques that create a favorable environment in which they can write and spell.

You have a crucial role to play. Much of what needs to be done will depend on school boards and administrators freeing teachers _from_ programs and _for_ children. Teachers must be free to place a new value on writing. Children must be free to spell without fear and receive encouragement as writers.

There is so much school boards and administrators can do. Here are just a few suggestions:

-- Support a child-centered curriculum.

-- Promote genuine interest in children's writing.

-- Involve teachers in decision-making about writing and spelling.

-- Establish frameworks, but don't impose materials or programs on teachers.

-- Keep both yourselves and your teachers informed of new understandings of spelling and writing development.

-- Support teachers' professional growth.

-- Promote parent involvement in schooling.

We can have proper spelling without pain. The answer lies in teachers who observe, understand, and promote children as learners.

Sincerely,

Richard Gentry

J. Richard Gentry

Dear Teacher,

My teachers in grade school must have been very pleased with my spelling. I passed weekly spelling test after weekly spelling test with the highest possible marks. But they wouldn't have been so pleased if they had realized I didn't know how to spell, in spite of my "success." They should have known. Looking at my writing, they should have been puzzled about why the words I spelled correctly on their spelling tests were misspelled in my compositions. But I can't remember them ever making a connection. So they never knew that I spent many hours preparing for their spelling tests, helped by my fabulous grandmother. She knew I couldn't spell!

My teachers depended on spelling materials and spelling tests. They graded, and unwittingly degraded! Their lesson plans for spelling basically moved kids through a set of materials.

Because I so sincerely want to prevent other kids from feeling the way I did, I'm asking you to re-examine your assumptions about spelling. If you still harbor some of the myths discussed in this book, perhaps it's time for you to form a new set of attitudes that will get you "back to the basics." And nothing in education is more basic than the freedom to teach and the freedom to learn.

What you do in your classroom will make the difference. I ask you to put your children before the mastery of spelling: recognize individual differences; hone your observational skills; make the children's spelling growth, not their completion of spelling books, your goal.

Here are some questions you should think about:

-- Is your classroom a place where children are free to learn?

-- Do you allow your children to choose the content and materials of their reading, writing, and spelling? Children need freedom to make decisions about literacy. Choices give them ownership.

-- Do your children make their own decisions about the writing process: what they should write, share, edit, rewrite, proofread? Choices in how and what to write are part of the learning process. Choices related to audience, genre, treatment, and length are at the heart of composing.

-- Are your children free to decide when they should worry about spelling? Children need choices in how to deal with spelling. They need more guidance and fewer commands.

-- Are your children free to grow in their own directions?

-- Do you respect your children's individual differences?

The real question behind all the others is this: Are your children free to _spell_, not just study about it? You must not _make_ them spell, but _free_ them to. You can better spend the energy you would use forcing children to spell in enticing them to do so of their own volition. Think about all the drills, all the worksheets and exercises, all the words memorized for tests. Think about all the poor grades, all the embarrassment, all the anxiety -- these are not the things that will free kids to spell.

On behalf of your children, I'm asking you to do the following:

-- Know the basics. Understand how kids learn to spell.

-- Shape your environment into one that facilitates the learning of spelling.

-- Open the doors that lead spellers deeper into the world of print. Get the kids to develop their interest in words, and to enjoy writing.

-- Ensure that the kids' spelling and writing lead to self-fulfillment, as well as to spelling and literacy development.

These things done, freedom and literacy leap, and children become the best spellers they can be.

Sincerely,

Richard Gentry

J. Richard Gentry

Dear Children,

When I was a kid, I had a lot of trouble with spelling. Actually, I could read what I wrote and so could everybody else. The problem was adults. Adults have trouble knowing how to react to poor spelling. You know how a cat's fur will stand up if you lock it in a room with a German shepherd. Many adults get <u>their</u> fur up when they see misspellings. There's nothing really disgusting or gross about misspelled words, but adults <u>think</u> they are bad. And since it's pretty hard to change the way adults think, here are a few tips for keeping your German shepherds (bad spellings) away from your cats (irritated adults).

Make an honest attempt to spell werds wright. Right the write werd when you no it. When u dont', hook it up. (That is, hook up your computer, type in your message, and turn on the spelling check.)

Don't feel bad if you're a terrible speller. Bad spellers can do almost <u>anything</u>. For proof, just look at this list of bad spellers: Queen Elizabeth I, George Washington, Andrew Jackson, Thomas Edison, Albert Einstein, Bruce Jenner, Cher. <u>Bad spellers can be successful!</u>

Learning to spell may not be as hard as you think. Like learning to speak, you get better by just doing it. Reading and writing are good for spelling, so write and read a lot and watch your spelling get better. Even if you find it hard to spell the words, keep writing.

While you're writing, don't worry about your spelling mistakes. Get your ideas down first, then when you need it, get some help with your spelling -- from dictionaries, friends, parents, teachers.

Keep in mind that good spelling is like good manners -- when others need to read what you've written, make sure you're on your best behavior.

Sincerely,

Richard Gentry

Richard Gentry

References

Carroll, J., P. Davies and B. Richman. *American Heritage Word Frequency Book.* Boston: Houghton Mifflin Company and American Heritage Publishing Company, 1971.

Dale, E. and J. O'Rourke. *The Living Word Vocabulary.* Chicago: World Book Inc., 1981.

Dewey, J. *The Child and the Curriculum.* Chicago: University of Chicago Press, 1902.

Fitzsimmons, R. and B. Loomer. *Spelling Research and Practice.* Iowa State Department of Public Instruction and University of Iowa, 1977.

Gentry, J.R. "An analysis of developmental spelling in GYNS AT WRK" in *Reading Teacher* 36, 192-200, 1982.

Greene, H.A. *The New Iowa Spelling Scale.* Iowa City: University of Iowa, 1954.

Hanna, P., J. Hanna, R. Hodges and E. Rudorf. *Phoneme Grapheme Correspondences as Cues to Spelling Improvement.* Washington: U.S. Government Printing Office, 1966.

Harris, A.J. and M.D. Jacobson. *Basic Elementary Reading Vocabularies.* New York: Macmillan, 1972.

Thomas, V. *Teaching Spelling: Canadian Word Lists and Instructional Techniques.* Toronto: Gage Educational Publishing Limited, 1979.

Other books in this series

In *Bright Idea* books, gifted authors reveal to readers the hearts of their professional lives. What has excited them professionally? What have they spent their years discovering? And why?

In these books they dress some old truths in new styles, and reveal some new truths about children, about language, about learning, about teachers, teaching, and parenting.

The series was conceived and is published in Canada, but the authors come from everywhere: the United States, New Zealand, The Netherlands, Great Britain, Canada.

So far seven titles have been published:

* ☞ **The Craft of Children's Writing**	Judith Newman
Learning Computer Learning	Veronica Buckley and Martin Lamb
Other Countries, Other Schools	Mike Bruce
* ☞ **Spel . . . Is a Four-Letter Word**	J. Richard Gentry
* **The Tone of Teaching**	Max van Manen
* ☞ **What's Whole in Whole Language?**	Ken Goodman
A Word Is a Word . . . Or Is It?	Michael Graves

In Canada, order from Scholastic-TAB Publications Ltd., 123 Newkirk Road, Richmond Hill, Ontario L4C 3G5.

* In the United States, order from Heinemann Educational Books, Inc., 70 Court Street, Portsmouth, NH 03801.

☞ Available in New Zealand and Australia through Ashton-Scholastic.